LET'S-READ-AND-FIND-OUT SCIENCE®

STAGE 2

Why Are the
ICE CAPS MELTING?

The Dangers of Global Warming

By Anne Rockwell • Illustrated by Paul Meisel

Collins
An Imprint of HarperCollinsPublishers

Special thanks to Mark A. Cane, G. Unger Vetlesen Professor of Earth and Climate Sciences, Lamont-Doherty Earth Observatory of Columbia University, for his valuable assistance.

The *Let's-Read-and-Find-Out Science* book series was originated by Dr. Franklyn M. Branley, Astronomer Emeritus and former Chairman of the American Museum–Hayden Planetarium, and was formerly co-edited by him and Dr. Roma Gans, Professor Emeritus of Childhood Education, Teachers College, Columbia University. Text and illustrations for each of the books in the series are checked for accuracy by an expert in the relevant field. For more information about Let's-Read-and-Find-Out Science books, write to HarperCollins Children's Books, 1350 Avenue of the Americas, New York, NY 10019, or visit our website at www.letsreadandfindout.com.

Library of Congress Cataloging-in-Publication Data
Rockwell, Anne F.
    Why are the ice caps melting? : the dangers of global warming / by Anne Rockwell ; illustrated by Paul Meisel. — 1st ed.
        p.   cm. — (Let's-read-and-find-out-science)
    ISBN-10: 0-06-054669-7 (trade bdg.) — ISBN-13: 978-0-06-054669-4 (trade bdg.)
    ISBN-10: 0-06-054671-9 (pbk.) — ISBN-13: 978-0-06-054671-7 (pbk.)
    1. Global warming—Juvenile literature. 2. Greenhouse effect, Atmospheric—Juvenile literature. I. Meisel, Paul, ill. II. Title. III. Series: Let's-read-and-find-out science book.
QC981.8.G56R63 2006   2005017972
363.738'74 —dc22

Typography by Elynn Cohen 2 3 4 5 6 7 8 9 10 ❖ First Edition

For my grandchildren
—A.R.

For all those who have dedicated their
lives to protecting the environment
—P.M.

Planet Earth, where we live, is a remarkable place. As far as scientists are able to tell, this small planet is the only place in the vast universe filled with other planets and stars that has plants and animals. That's because Earth may be the only place where the conditions are just right for living things to exist.

All the different kinds of plants and animals on Earth need an environment that is just right for their needs. Among the things they need in their environment is just the right amount of warmth. If it's too hot or too cold, they can't survive. Many scientists have found evidence in recent years that our planet is growing warmer—too warm, in fact. They call this global warming.

The earth is surrounded by a layer of gases called the atmosphere. Some of the gas is water vapor. The other gases are carbon dioxide, methane, nitrous oxide, and fluorocarbons. These gases form an invisible cover that holds the heat of the sun. Scientists call this the "greenhouse effect." That's because the gases work something like the glass of a greenhouse. They let in sunlight and keep the sun's warmth from escaping too quickly.

Everything in nature must be in balance—not too much and not too little. The earth needs just the right amount of the greenhouse effect to be warm enough for living things. But if too much greenhouse gas surrounds the earth, the sun's heat can't escape. The earth will become too warm.

It's too warm for these plants in the greenhouse.

Many different things in nature make carbon dioxide. Human beings and other animals put some carbon dioxide into the atmosphere every time they exhale, or breathe out. Burning coal and oil and automobile gasoline makes much more. Power plants that give us electricity use oil and coal. We also use oil and coal to heat our stores, homes, schools, and offices. Garbage rotting in landfills makes methane gas. Nitrous oxide is released into the atmosphere when we mine coal and dig for oil or natural gas. Fluorocarbons are released when we use some aerosol sprays—these are illegal in many countries now.

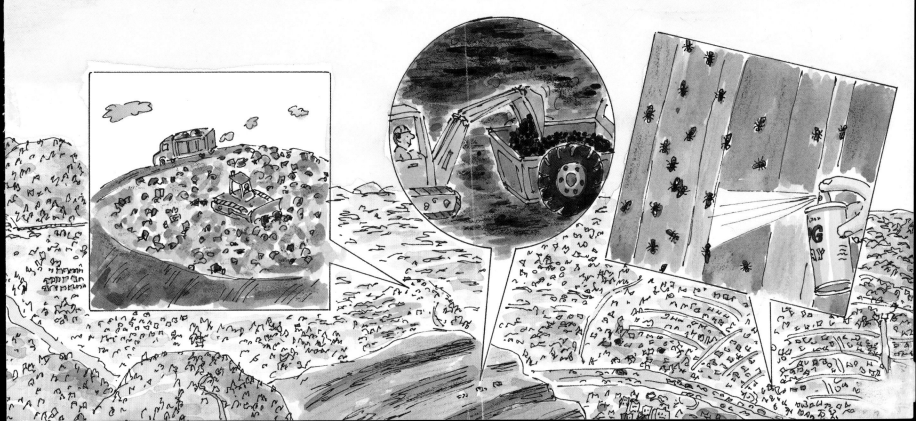

The trouble is that today there are many, many people on Earth driving cars, going to school, working in offices and factories, throwing out their garbage, and using aerosols. These things make the greenhouse layer thicker. This means less heat escapes from the earth, so every year the earth grows warmer and warmer.

It has gotten so warm that the huge ice shelf at the South Pole and the land glaciers in the Arctic are melting. As this ice melts, it falls into the sea. The sea grows deeper.

There is no place for this extra water to go, so sea levels are rising.

Scientists all over the world have been measuring average tides. Tides are only a few inches higher now, but if they continue to rise at the same rate, a great deal of land will be underwater or in danger of flooding during big storms. People and land animals will have less land to live on.

Scientists also measure temperatures all over the world. They find that the average temperatures worldwide are getting higher. This means that now it is warm enough for animals, insects, and plants that can live only in warm climates to move into new territories. Mockingbirds that lived only in the southern United States are now regularly spotted in New England, and some migratory birds such as robins can be found in their summer territories year-round.

As the earth grows warmer and warmer, rivers will dry up. More and more land will be covered with deserts, with little water for farming.

Does this sound like bad news to you? It does to scientists. The vast majority of them believe that people cause global warming, so people must help stop it.

Some people say we don't cause global warming. They say that the earth's climate has changed many times in the past. It has grown warmer or colder, and many great and drastic changes in temperature happened before there were any people on the earth. They say that since we don't know what caused those changes, we don't really know what's causing the changes that are taking place now.

But even if what these people say turns out to be true, it's still a good idea for us to do whatever we can to try to stop the amount of greenhouse gases from increasing.

One way to help stop global warming is by planting trees.

People and animals breathe in oxygen and breathe out carbon dioxide. We're always making the greenhouse layer thicker. But green plants help maintain the balance of the greenhouse layer. They turn carbon dioxide into oxygen. That way there is less carbon dioxide. If highways had trees on both sides, some of the carbon dioxide that car engines make would be turned into oxygen by those trees. That carbon dioxide wouldn't add to the greenhouse effect. The same is true of factories and cities and towns. Parks in big cities wouldn't only look pretty. They would also help the earth.

Much of the warmest part of the earth, which lies on either side of the equator, is covered by dense rain forests. The trees in these hot and steamy ancient forests produce most of the oxygen human beings and other animals need to live.

But today these forests are being cut down to make lumber for houses and other buildings and wood pulp for paper. They're being cut down so fast that new trees don't have a chance to grow. People then burn the leaves and branches, which releases more carbon dioxide into the air.

Plankton

The surface of the ocean is covered with a layer of plants and animals so small you can see them only with a microscope. This layer of living things is called plankton. It is food for many larger sea animals.

The tiny plants of plankton do something besides feed great whales. They turn carbon dioxide into oxygen, just as trees do. Since so much of the earth's surface is covered with ocean, tiny plankton plants convert a lot of carbon dioxide into oxygen.

But this could change. If too much freshwater enters the sea from melting polar ice, the sea's environment will change. Not all plankton will survive the change. That will mean even more carbon dioxide will not be changed into oxygen and will add to the greenhouse effect. The earth will grow warmer and warmer, and it will happen faster and faster.

Does all this sound scary? Most scientists think it's very scary indeed. They say all the people in the world, and all the industrial nations of the world, must work together now to stop global warming. They say we must work quickly.

What can you and I do to help?

We can plant trees. We can stop using aerosol sprays and use pump sprays instead. We can buy appliances that are designed to use less energy and tell us that by the seal pasted on them.

We can walk or bicycle to places that aren't far away. We can write letters at home and at school to representatives in Congress, telling them that we think global warming matters.

AIR CONDITIONER SALE

Energy ✬ Saving ✬ Model ✬

Energy Efficient $249. annual savings

HYBRID FUEL ECONOMY 38 city 45 highway

Dear Congressman,
Please help limit greenhouse gases.
Sincerely,
Julie

We can keep our houses, schools, stores, and workplaces cooler in the winter and use the air conditioner less in the summer. We can turn off our TV sets, computers, and lights when we aren't using them. When we do these things, we use less oil and natural gas in our furnaces. Power plants don't have to burn as much coal and oil to make electricity for our air conditioners, TV sets, computers, and lights.

We can buy foods that aren't prepackaged, because all those paper packages are made from trees. If we used fewer packages, we wouldn't put as much garbage in our landfills. Less methane gas would be made. We can recycle.

Turn off the lights, Rusty.

We must also help by learning more and more about nature on this remarkable planet where we live. Some of you may learn enough to want to become scientists who spend their lives studying the earth and what lives on it. The more we know, the more ways we will find to keep our earth and us and all the earth's other living things alive and healthy.

The Greenhouse Effect

To learn more about how the greenhouse effect works, try going to a real greenhouse—maybe you live near a botanical garden or a garden center. Bring a thermometer with you.

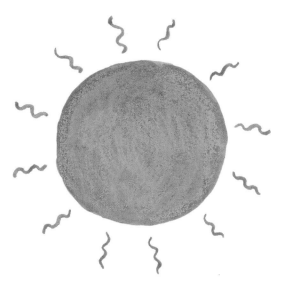

First take the temperature outside the greenhouse and write it down. Then take the temperature inside.

How are they different? Why do you think the indoor temperature is higher?

Earth's atmosphere works just like the ceiling of a greenhouse. The heat and light come in right through the glass, but it is much harder for them to get out. That's why the temperature inside a greenhouse is higher.

Warmer temperatures don't exist only in greenhouses. Earth's average temperature has risen 1 degree Fahrenheit in the last 100 years. Though this seems to be a small change, a continued increase (or decrease) in temperature could dramatically change Earth's climate. In the last ice age, most of North America was covered by a glacier and the average temperature of Earth was only 7 degrees Fahrenheit colder than today!

What Can You Do?

Think about the things you do every day, from waking up to brushing your teeth at night. Some of the things you do produce greenhouse gases, and some don't.

Over the course of a day, make a list of the things you do that produce greenhouse gases:

1. What things do you do that use electricity? How many hours a day do you spend

   watching television?

   playing video games?

   using a computer?

   listening to the stereo?

   What do you think you could use less of to

   help the environment? How many fun

   activities can you think of that don't produce any

   greenhouse gases?

2. Keep a log of all the garbage you throw away—even if it's just a candy bar wrapper. At the end of the day, look at your list and imagine how big a pile your garbage would make. Can you think of three ways to reduce this pile?

Can you think of any other ways to keep track of how you affect the environment? There might be something not on these lists!